Stranded at O'Hare

Other Books by Kelly Warnken

The Information Brokers

So You Want to be an Information Broker?

Stranded at O'Hare

by Kelly Warnken

The Book Factory, Inc.
Chicago, Illinois

Copyright © 1993
by Kelly Warnken

First printing 1993
Printed in the United States of America

All rights reserved including the
right of reproduction in whole or
in part in any form without written
permission from the author, except
for the inclusion of brief quotations
in a review.

Published by

The Book Factory, Inc.
Chicago, IL

ISBN # 1-883603-00-5

Dedicated to

Michael J. Polelle

TABLE OF CONTENTS

Preface	ix
Why You Need This Book	1
Hotels	3
Restaurants	47
Transportation	63
Airlines	69
Business Services	71
Entertainment	73
Recreational Sports	79
Shopping	85
Practical Information	87
Emergencies	89

PREFACE

As a business traveler and former airline employee I have spent many hours waiting in airports. When I'm trapped in an airport I often have the feeling that I'm missing something interesting nearby—an ethnic restaurant, a friendly night spot—a place that only the locals know about. Travel guidebooks are of little help: they only tease with enticing descriptions of sights and activities too far away to enjoy. Seldom are airports located near city centers or quaint neighborhoods. My frustration with airports led me to compile this unusual book.

STRANDED AT O'HARE is no ordinary guidebook. This is a traveller's guide to the area that surrounds O'Hare International Airport. We native Chicagoans call this "The Land Beyond O'Hare". Like most of the Midwest it is flat but it is a rich resource for travellers who need food, a place to sleep and an antidote to boredom. I've also tried to provide solutions to other problems such as running short of cash, a midnight toothache and finding an all night pharmacy near O'Hare.

While business travellers can choose from many travel guides, only **STRANDED AT O'HARE** was written with the needs of "grounded passengers" in mind; business travellers' needs change when forced by outside circumstances. Proximity to O'Hare becomes crucial. What good is knowing about a top rated Chicago restaurant if you can't get back to the airport in time to make your flight? And to the reluctant traveller who arrives at 2:00 am, an ordinary hotel that offers 24 hour room service is more enticing than a famous hotel with curtailed hours.

Travelling short distances from O'Hare should not be difficult or expensive but to someone unfamiliar with the local transportation system the choices can be overwhelming. For example, cab rates vary according to where the operator's vehicle is licensed. Choosing the best mode of transportation depends on a traveler's knowledge of the vagaries of the local transportation system and the traveler's personal preferences. For some people riding in the back of a limo is the only way to go while others are delighted to save money by taking the subway from O'Hare.

Because Chicago is the nation's transportation center, passengers can take advantage of other airports, cross country busses and nationwide railroad service.

Note: Every care has been taken to verify the accuracy of the information presented. But in today's world, prices change and businesses move or close their doors. In any event, it's always a good idea to call ahead to verify prices, availability of services and hours of operation.

WHY YOU NEED THIS BOOK

If you're one of 64 million people who pass through O'Hare International Airport each year or one of 30 million passengers making connections you probably think being **STRANDED AT O'HARE** means boredom and frustration. Well, you're in for a surprise! An exciting world lies just *outside* the airport.

Remember the last time you were **STRANDED AT O'HARE?** What did you do? Maybe you drank a cocktail or ate a hot dog—and you waited and waited and waited. Well, here are some of the things you could be doing the next time you're **STRANDED AT O'HARE.**

1. Munch on a slab of ribs at Chicago's #1 rib restaurant.
2. Play night golf at a 9 hole lighted golf course.
3. Swim in an Olympic size pool.
4. Attend a thoroughbred horse race.

5. Eat caviar and drink vodka in a Russian nightclub.

Pack this little book in your suitcase and you'll see that being **STRANDED AT O'HARE** can **BE FUN!**

HOTELS

Damn! The next flight isn't until tomorrow and it looks like you're going to be **STRANDED AT O'HARE** overnight. So, like it or not, you must find a hotel.

The **O'Hare Hilton,** the only hotel on O'Hare property, is located a short walk from the runways. This newly renovated hotel is a popular site for business conferences and it fills up quickly when flights are delayed. It doesn't take a genius to figure out that O'Hare's daily load of over 175,000 passengers can't squeeze into the hotel's 855 rooms on a stormy night.

Fortunately there are many other options; hotels near O'Hare can meet the needs of any traveller made weary by a journey gone wrong. What kind of hotel amenities are you looking for? Do you want a refreshing swim and a strenuous workout in a health club? Or would you enjoy a cocktail in an elegant lobby lounge followed by a delicious room service meal? And, of course, the hotel should be close to O'Hare so that you don't miss your flight in the morning.

To select a hotel you could join the hordes of stranded passengers at the hotel information boards near the luggage carrousels, read the advertisements, then scramble for a chance to use a courtesy phone. Or you could take your copy of **STRANDED AT O'HARE** to a quiet telephone bank on the departure level. (Don't be deceived by the tiny billboards into thinking that these are the only hotels near O'Hare, **STRANDED AT O'HARE** lists four times as many hotels.)

The hotel listings in this book are easy to read. Arranged by location—within 5 miles, within 10 miles, within 15 miles and downtown Chicago—each entry includes a brief listing of some of the hotel's features: swimming pool (indoor or outdoor), health club, cocktail lounge and restaurant. Rates quoted are for one person staying in a standard room or suite (tax not included).

Approximate prices are quoted for taxis, vans and public transportation. If the hotel you select provides a courtesy car for guests, ask a hotel staff member if the service is free. At some hotels "courtesy" doesn't mean "complimentary", it means a charge of up to $15 per person. For more information on saving money on transportation to your hotel, take a minute or two to read the chapter on transportation.

Hotels in the Airport

There is only one hotel in the airport.

O'HARE HILTON
O'Hare International Airport
Opposite Terminal #2   312 686-8000
Chicago, IL   800 HILTONS

Cost: Single Rate $155
Features: Restaurant, lounge, health club. No Pool.
Transportation: Walk to Lower Level Terminal #2

Hotels within 5 Miles of O'Hare

BEST WESTERN AT O'HARE
10300 W Higgins Rd
Rosemont, IL

708 296-4471
800 528-1234

Cost: Single Rate $68–85
Features: Restaurant, lounge, outdoor pool. For a nominal fee hotel guests may use a health club and indoor pool near the hotel.
Transportation: Courtesy van from O'Hare

BEST WESTERN MIDWAY HOTEL
1600 Oakton St
Elk Grove Village, IL

708 981-0010
800 528-1234

Cost: Single Rate $54–$74
Features: Restaurant, lounge, indoor pool. No health club.
Transportation: Courtesy van from O'Hare

CHELSEA MOTOR INN
1275 Lee St
Des Plaines, IL

708 298-1700

Cost: Single Rate $32
Features: Restaurant, lounge. No health club or pool.
Transportation: Courtesy van from O'Hare

CLARION HOTEL
6810 N Mannheim Rd
Rosemont, IL

708 297-1234
800 221-2222

Cost: Single Rate $59–$92
Features: Restaurant, lounge, health club, indoor pool.
Transportation: Courtesy van from O'Hare

COMFORT INN O'HARE
2175 E Touhy Av 708 635-1300
Des Plaines, IL 800 221-2222
Cost: Single $52–$71
Features: Restaurant, lounge, health club. No pool.
Transportation: Courtesy van from O'Hare

COURTYARD BY MARRIOTT
2950 S River Rd 708 824-7000
Des Plaines, IL 800 321-2211
Cost: Single Rate $91
Features: Restaurant, lounge, indoor pool. No health club.
Transportation: Courtesy van from O'Hare

DAYS INN
1900 N Mannheim Rd 708 681-3100
Melrose Park, IL 800 325-2525
Cost: Single Rate $41–$47
Features: No restaurant or lounge. No health club or pool.
Transportation: Suburban Taxi from O'Hare $15

DAYS INN O'HARE SOUTH
3801 Mannheim Rd 708 678-0670
Schiller Park, IL 800 325-2525
Cost: Single Rate $60
Features: Restaurant, lounge, outdoor pool. No health club.
Transportation: Courtesy van from O'Hare

EMBASSY SUITES
6501 N Mannheim Rd 708 699-6300
Rosemont, IL 800 EMBASSY

Cost: Single Rate $150–$170
Features: Restaurant, lounge, health club, indoor pool.
Transportation: Courtesy van from O'Hare

EXEL INN
1000 W Devon Av 708 894-2085
Elk Grove Village, IL 800 356-8013

Cost: Single Rate $42–$45
Features: Restaurant and lounge near hotel. No health club or pool.
Transportation: Suburban Taxi from O'Hare $12

EXEL INN
2881 Touhy Av 708 803-9400
Elk Grove Village, IL 800 356-8013

Cost: Single Rate $39–43
Features: Restaurant and lounge near hotel. No health club or pool.
Transportation: Courtesy van from O'Hare

GRAND INN
3010 N Mannheim Rd
Franklin Park, IL 708 451-1400

Cost: Single Rate $47
Features: Restaurant and lounge near hotel. Health club. No pool.
Transportation: Courtesy van from O'Hare

HAMPTON INN
100 Busse Rd 708 593-8600
Elk Grove Village, IL 800 426-7866

Cost: Single Rate $55–$57
Features: Restaurant and lounge near hotel. No health club or pool.
Transportation: Courtesy van from O'Hare

HAMPTON INN

| 3939 N Mannheim Rd | 708 671-1700 |
| Schiller Park, IL | 800 426-7866 |

Cost: Single Rate $62
Features: Health club and outdoor pool. No restaurant or lounge.
Transportation: Courtesy van from O'Hare

HOLIDAY INN

| 1450 E Touhy Av | 708 296-8866 |
| Des Plaines, IL | 800 HOLIDAY |

Cost: Single Rate $79–$95
Features: Restaurant, lounge, health club, outdoor pool.
Transportation: Courtesy van from O'Hare

HOLIDAY INN

| 5440 N River Rd | 708 671-6350 |
| Rosemont, IL | 800 HOLIDAY |

Cost: Single Rate $97–$135
Features: Restaurant, lounge, health club, indoor pool.
Transportation: Courtesy van from O'Hare

HOWARD JOHNSON

| 5615 N Cumberland Av | 312 693-5800 |
| Chicago, IL | 800 IGOHOJO |

Cost: Single Rate $59–$109

Features: Restaurant, lounge, outdoor pool. No
  health club.
Transportation: Courtesy van from O'Hare

HOWARD JOHNSON O'HARE
8201 W Higgins Rd 312 693-2323
Chicago, IL 800 IGOHOJO

Cost: Single Rate $40–$50
Features: Restaurant, lounge, outdoor pool. No
  health club.
Transportation: Courtesy van from O'Hare

HOWARD JOHNSON
10249 Irving Park Rd 708 671-6000
Schiller Park, IL 800 IGOHOJO

Cost: Single Rate $45–$101
Features: Restaurant, health club, indoor pool.
  Lounge near hotel.
Transportation: Courtesy van from O'Hare

HYATT REGENCY O'HARE
9300 W Bryn Mawr Av 708 696-1234
Rosemont, IL 800 233-1234

Cost: Single Rate $155–$170
Features: Restaurant, lounge, 24 hr room service,
  health club, indoor pool.
Transportation: Courtesy van from O'Hare

LA QUINTA INN
1900 E Oakton St. 708 439-6767
Elk Grove Village, IL 800 531-5900

Cost: Single Rate $52–$59
Features: Restaurant, lounge and health club near
  hotel. Outdoor pool.
Transportation: Courtesy van from O'Hare

MARRIOTT O'HARE
8535 W Higgins Rd 312 693-4444
Chicago, IL 800 228-9290

Cost: Single Rate $145
Features: Restaurant, lounge, health club, indoor pool.
Transportation: Courtesy van from O'Hare

MARRIOTT SUITES
6155 N River Rd 708 696-4400
Rosemont, IL 800 228-9290

Cost: Single Rate $160
Features: Restaurant, lounge, health club, indoor pool.
Transportation: Courtesy van from O'Hare

QUALITY INN
6810 N Mannheim Rd 708 297-1234
Rosemont, IL 800 221-2222

Cost: Single Rate $49–$78
Features: Restaurant, lounge, health club, indoor pool.
Transportation: Courtesy van from O'Hare

RADISSON SUITE HOTEL O'HARE
5500 River Rd 708 678-4000
Rosemont, IL 800 333-3333

Cost: Single Rate $135–$150
Features: Restaurant, lounge, health club, indoor pool.
Transportation: Courtesy van from O'Hare

RAMADA
6600 N Mannheim Rd 708 827-5131
Rosemont, IL 800 2-RAMADA

Cost: Single Rate $96–$118
Features: Restaurant, lounge, health club, indoor pool.
Transportation: Courtesy van from O'Hare

RESIDENCE INN BY MARRIOTT
9450 Lawrence Av	708 678-2210
Schiller Park, IL	800 331-3131

Cost: Single Rate $119
Features: Restaurant and lounge near hotel. Outdoor pool. For a nominal fee hotel guests may use a health club near the hotel.
Transportation: Courtesy van from O'Hare

SOFITEL HOTEL
5550 N River Rd	708 678-4488
Rosemont, IL	800 233-5959

Cost: Single Rate $89–$159
Features: Restaurant, lounge, health club, indoor pool.
Transportation: Courtesy van from O'Hare

TRAVELODGE
3003 Mannheim Rd	708 296-5541
Des Plaines, IL	800 255-3050

Cost: Single Rate $49–$70
Features: Outdoor pool. Restaurant and lounge near hotel. No health club.
Transportation: Any taxi from O'Hare $12

WESTIN HOTEL O'HARE
6100 N River Rd	708 698-6000
Rosemont, IL	800 228-3000

Cost: Single Rate $145–$165

Features: Restaurant, lounge, health club, indoor pool.
Transportation: Courtesy van from O'Hare

Hotels within 10 Miles of O'Hare

BEST WESTERN ARLINGTON INN
948 E Northwest Hwy	708 255-2900
Arlington Heights, IL	800 528-1234

Cost: Single Rate $45–$75
Features: Restaurant, lounge, health club, indoor pool.
Transportation: Courtesy van from O'Hare

BEST WESTERN BRADBURY SUITES
2111 S Arlington Heights Rd	708 956-1400
Arlington Heights, IL	800 528-1234

Cost: Single Rate $45–$75
Features: Restaurant. Lounge near hotel. No health club or pool.
Transportation: Suburban Taxi from O'Hare $15

BEST WESTERN INN OF LAGRANGE
5631 S La Grange Rd	708 352-2480
La Grange, IL	800 528-1234

Cost: Single Rate $42–$58
Features: Restaurant and lounge near hotel. Outdoor pool. No health club.
Transportation: Suburban Taxi from O'Hare $22

BEST WESTERN MORTON GROVE INN
9424 Waukegan Rd	708 965-6400
Morton Grove, IL	800 528-1234

Cost: Single Rate $32–$50
Features: Restaurant and lounge near hotel. No health club or pool.
Transportation: Suburban Taxi from O'Hare $17

BEST WESTERN SCHAUMBURG
1725 E Algonquin Rd   708 397-1500
Schaumburg, IL   800 528-1234

Cost: Single Rate $55
Features: Restaurant, lounge, outdoor pool. No health club.
Transportation: Courtesy van from O'Hare

CARLETON OF OAK PARK
1110 Pleasant St
Oak Park, IL   708 848-5000

Cost: Single Rate $56–$79
Features: Restaurant, lounge, health club. No pool.
Transportation: Any taxi from O'Hare $16

COMFORT INN
2550 Landmeier Rd   708 364-6200
Elk Grove Village, IL   800 221-2222

Cost: Single Rate $49
Features: Restaurant and lounge. No health club or pool.
Transportation: Suburban Taxi from O'Hare $12

COMFORT INN
370 N Rt 83   708 941-9444
Elmhurst, IL   800 221-2222

Cost: Single Rate $59–$89
Features: Restaurant near hotel. Health club, indoor pool.
Transportation: Suburban Taxi from O'Hare $17

COMFORT INN
2801 Algonquin Rd   708 259-5900
Rolling Meadows, IL   800 221-2222

Cost: Single Rate $50–$75
Features: Restaurant near hotel. Outdoor pool. No health club.
Transportation: Suburban Taxi from O'Hare $18

COURTYARD BY MARRIOTT
100 W Algonquin Rd   708 437-3344
Arlington Heights, IL   800 321-2211

Cost: Single Rate $65
Features: Restaurant, lounge, health club, indoor pool.
Transportation: Suburban Taxi from O'Hare $15

COURTYARD BY MARRIOTT
1801 Milwaukee Av   708 803-2500
Glenview, IL   800 321-2211

Cost: Single Rate $49
Features: Restaurant, lounge, indoor pool. No health club.
Transportation: Suburban Taxi from O'Hare $14, Airport Express $13.75

COURTYARD BY MARRIOTT
6 Trans Am Plaza Dr   708 691-1500
Oak Brook Terrace, IL   800 321-2211

Cost: Single Rate $49
Features: Restaurant, lounge, indoor pool. No health club.
Transportation: Suburban Taxi from O'Hare $17

COURTYARD BY MARRIOTT
900 Wood Dale Rd   708 766-7775

HOTELS 15

Wood Dale, IL   800 321-2211

Cost: Single Rate $49
Features: Restaurant, lounge, indoor pool. No health club.
Transportation: Suburban Taxi from O'Hare $17

DAYS INN
600 E Lake St   708 834-8800
Addison, IL   800 325-2525

Cost: Single Rate $38
Features: Health club. No restaurant, lounge, or pool.
Transportation: Suburban Taxi from O'Hare $25

DAYS INN
6450 W Touhy Av   708 647-7700
Niles, IL   800 325-2525

Cost: Single Rate $47–$101
Features: Restaurant and lounge near hotel. No health club or pool.
Transportation: Any taxi from O'Hare $15

DOUBLE TREE CLUB HOTEL
800 National Pkwy   708 605-9222
Schaumburg, IL

Cost: Single Rate $49–$85
Features: Restaurant, lounge, health club, indoor pool.
Transportation: Suburban Taxi from O'Hare $17

EMBASSY SUITES
707 E Butterfield Rd   708 969-7500
Lombard, IL   800 EMBASSY

Cost: Single Rate $113–$144
Features: Restaurant, lounge, health club, indoor pool
Transportation: Courtesy van from O'Hare

EXEL INN
540 Milwaukee Av   708 459-0545
Prospect Heights, IL   800 356-8013
Cost: Single Rate $29–$35
Features: Restaurant and lounge near hotel. For a nominal fee hotel guests may use a health club near the hotel.
Transportation: Suburban Taxi from O'Hare $26

FAIRFIELD INN
4514 W Lake Av   708 299-1600
Glenview, IL   800 228-2800
Cost: Single Rate $42–$49
Features: Restaurant and lounge near hotel. Outdoor pool. No health club.
Transportation: Suburban Taxi from O'Hare $14, Airport Express $13.75

FOREST LODGE
1246 S River Rd
Prospect Heights, IL   708 537-2000
Cost: Single Rate $29–$32
Features: Restaurant and lounge. No health club or pool.
Transportation: Suburban Taxi from O'Hare $26

HAMPTON INN
222 E 22nd St   708 916-9000
Lombard, IL   800 426-7866

Cost: Single Rate $52–$55
Features: Restaurant and lounge near hotel. Health club. No pool.
Transportation: Suburban Taxi from O'Hare $17

HAMPTON INN
1300 E Higgins Rd
Schaumburg, IL
708 619-1000
800 426-7866

Cost: Single Rate $58–$60
Features: Restaurant and lounge near hotel. Health club. No pool.
Transportation: Suburban Taxi from O'Hare $15

HAMPTON INN
2222 Enterprise Dr
Westchester, IL
708 409-1000
800 426-7866

Cost: Single Rate $53–$58
Features: Restaurant and lounge near hotel. Health club. No pool.
Transportation: Suburban Taxi from O'Hare $17

HILTON & TOWERS – WOODFIELD
3400 W Euclid Av
Arlington Heights, IL
708 394-2000
800 HILTONS

Cost: Single Rate $105–$135
Features: Restaurant, lounge, health club, indoor pool.
Transportation: Courtesy van from O'Hare

HOLIDAY INN
1000 Busse Rd
Elk Grove Village, IL
708 437-6010
800 HOLIDAY

Cost: Single Rate $80–$90

Features: Restaurant, lounge, health club, indoor pool.

Transportation: Courtesy van from O'Hare

HOLIDAY INN
624 York Rd 708 279-1100
Elmhurst, IL 800 HOLIDAY

Cost: Single Rate $75–$82
Features: Restaurant, lounge, health club, indoor pool.
Transportation: Courtesy van from O'Hare

HOLIDAY INN
4400 Frontage Rd 708 544-9300
Hillside, IL 800 HOLIDAY

Cost: Single Rate $69
Features: Restaurant, lounge, health club. No pool.
Transportation: Suburban Taxi from O'Hare $25

HOLIDAY INN
860 Irving Park Rd 708 773-2340
Itasca, IL 800 HOLIDAY

Cost: Single Rate $62–$78
Features: Restaurant, lounge, health club, indoor pool.
Transportation: Suburban Taxi from O'Hare $12

HOLIDAY INN
200 E Rand Rd 708 255-8800
Mt. Prospect, IL 800 HOLIDAY

Cost: Single Rate $47–$59
Features: Restaurant and lounge. Health club and indoor pool near hotel.
Transportation: Courtesy van from O'Hare

HOLIDAY INN
Rts 62 and 53   708 259-5000
Rolling Meadows, IL   800 HOLIDAY

Cost: Single Rate $79
Features: Restaurant, lounge, health club, indoor pool.
Transportation: Courtesy van from O'Hare

HOLIDAY INN
5300 W Touhy Av   708 679-8900
Skokie, IL   800 HOLIDAY

Cost: Single Rate $89–$99
Features: Restaurant, lounge, health club, indoor pool.
Transportation: Suburban Taxi from O'Hare $18, Airport Express $13.75

HOLIDAY INN CROWNE PLAZA
2855 N Milwaukee Av   708 480-7500
Northbrook, IL   800 HOLIDAY

Cost: Single Rate $100–$105
Features: Restaurant, lounge, health club, indoor pool.
Transportation: Courtesy van from O'Hare, Airport Express $13.75

HOLIDAY INN EXPRESS
2120 S Arlington Heights Rd   708 593-9400
Arlington Heights, IL   800 HOLIDAY

Cost: Single Rate $49–$54
Features: Restaurant and lounge near hotel. No health club or pool.
Transportation: Suburban Taxi from O'Hare $15

HOLIDAY INN EXPRESS
933 S Riverside Dr   708 279-0700
Elmhurst, IL   800 HOLIDAY

Cost: Single Rate $65

Features: Restaurant and lounge near hotel. Health club and outdoor pool.

Transportation: Suburban Taxi from O'Hare $17

HYATT REGENCY
1800 E Golf Rd   708 605-1234
Schaumburg, IL   800 233-1234

Cost: Single Rate $155–$170

Features: Restaurant, lounge, health club, outdoor pool.

Transportation: Suburban Taxi from O'Hare $15

LA QUINTA INN
1730 E Higgins Rd   708 517-8484
Schaumburg, IL   800 531-5900

Cost: Single Rate $51–$65

Features: Lounge, health club and 24 hour restaurant near hotel. Outdoor pool.

Transportation: Suburban Taxi from O'Hare $15

MARRIOTT
1401 W 22nd St   708 573-8555
Oak Brook, IL   800 228-9290

Cost: Single Rate $69–$135

Features: Restaurant, lounge, health club, indoor pool.

Transportation: Suburban Taxi from O'Hare $17

MARRIOTT
50 N Martingale Rd   708 240-0100
Schaumburg, IL   800 228-9290

Cost: Single Rate $115–$135
Features: Restaurant, lounge, health club, indoor pool.
Transportation: Suburban Taxi from O'Hare $15

MARRIOTT SUITES
1500 Opus Pl   708 852-1500
Downers Grove, IL   800 228-9290

Cost: Single Rate $125
Features: Restaurant, lounge, health club, indoor pool.
Transportation: Suburban Taxi from O'Hare $20

NORDIC HILLS RESORT & CONFERENCE CENTER
Rt 53 and Nordic Rd   708 773-2750
Itasca, IL   800 334-3417

Cost: Single Rate $110–$115
Features: Restaurant, lounge, health club and indoor pool.
Transportation: Courtesy van from O'Hare

OMNI ORRINGTON HOTEL
1710 Orrington Av   708 866-8700
Evanston, IL   800 843-6664

Cost: Single Rate $110–$130
Features: Restaurant and lounge. For a nominal fee hotel guests may use Northwestern University's health club and indoor pool.
Transportation: Any taxi from O'Hare $25, Airport Express $13.75

QUALITY INN
10 W Roosevelt Rd   708 941-9100
Villa Park, IL   800 221-2222

Cost: Single Rate $40–$50
Features: Restaurant and lounge near hotel. Outdoor pool. No health club.
Transportation: Suburban Taxi from O'Hare $20

RADISSON
4500 Touhy Av 708 677-1234
Lincolnwood, IL 800 333-3333
Cost: Single Rate $79–$112
Features: Restaurant, lounge, health club, indoor pool.
Transportation: Any Taxi from O'Hare $16, Airport Express $13.75

RADISSON SUITE HOTEL GLENVIEW
1400 Milwaukee Av 708 803-9800
Glenview, IL 800 333-3333
Cost: Single Rate $98–$101
Features: Restaurant, lounge, health club, indoor pool.
Transportation: Suburban Taxi from O'Hare $14, Airport Express $13.75

RAMADA INN
2875 N Milwaukee Av 708 298-2525
Northbrook, IL 800 2-RAMADA
Cost: Single Rate $58–$66
Features: Restaurant, lounge, health club, outdoor pool.
Transportation: Courtesy van from O'Hare, Airport Express $13.75

RAMADA
17 W 350 22nd St 708 833-3600
Oak Brook Terrace, IL 800 2-RAMADA

Cost: Single Rate $62–$71
Features: Restaurant, lounge, health club, outdoor pool.
Transportation: Suburban Taxi from O'Hare $17

RED ROOF INN
I-90 & Arlington Heights Rd   708 228-6650
Arlington Heights, IL   800 THE ROOF

Cost: Single Rate $39
Features: Restaurant and lounge near hotel. No health club or pool.
Transportation: Suburban Taxi from O'Hare $15

RESIDENCE INN BY MARRIOTT
530 Lake Cook Rd   708 940-4644
Deerfield, IL   800 331-3131

Cost: Single Rate $69–$109
Features: Restaurant and lounge near hotel. Outdoor pool. No health club.
Transportation: Suburban Taxi from O'Hare $18, Airport Express $13.75

SHERATON SUITES
121 Northwest Point Blvd   708 290-1600
Elk Grove Village, IL   800 325-3535

Cost: Single Rate $79–$125
Features: Restaurant, lounge, health club, indoor pool.
Transportation: Suburban Taxi from O'Hare $12

TRAVELODGE
7247 N Waukegan Rd   708 647-9444
Niles, IL   800 255-3050

Cost: Single Rate $44–$52

Features: Restaurant and lounge near hotel. Outdoor pool. No health club.
Transportation: Any Taxi from O'Hare $15

WYNDHAM GARDEN HOTEL
1200 N Mittel Blvd   708 860-2900
Wood Dale, IL   800 822-4200

Cost: Single Rate $54–$89
Features: Restaurant and lounge. Indoor pool. No health club.
Transportation: Suburban Taxi from O'Hare $17

WYNDHAM HAMILTON HOTEL
400 Park Blvd   708 773-4000
Itasca, IL   800 822-4200

Cost: Single Rate $99–$179
Features: Restaurant, lounge, health club, indoor pool.
Transportation: Suburban Taxi from O'Hare $18

Hotels within 15 Miles of O'Hare

COMFORT INN
3010 Finley Rd   708 515-1500
Downers Grove, IL   800 221-2222

Cost: Single Rate $50–$75
Features: Restaurant and lounge near hotel. Outdoor pool. No health club.
Transportation: Suburban Taxi from O'Hare $20

COMFORT SUITES
17 W 445 Roosevelt Rd   708 916-1000
Oak Brook Terrace, IL   800 221-2222

Cost: Single Rate $49–$63
Features: Restaurant near hotel. Lounge, health club, indoor pool.
Transportation: Suburban Taxi from O'Hare $17

COURTYARD BY MARRIOTT
3700 N Wilke Rd 708 394-9999
Arlington Heights, IL 800 321-2211

Cost: Single Rate $56
Features: Restaurant, lounge, health club, indoor pool.
Transportation: Suburban Taxi from O'Hare $15

COURTYARD BY MARRIOTT
800 Lake Cook Rd 708 940-8222
Deerfield, IL 800 321-2211

Cost: Single Rate $56
Features: Restaurant, lounge, indoor pool. No health club.
Transportation: Suburban Taxi from O'Hare $18, Airport Express $13.75

THE DRAKE OAK BROOK
2301 York Rd 708 574-5700
Oak Brook, IL 800 334-9805

Cost: Single Rate $65–$110
Features: Restaurant and lounge. Indoor pool. Hotel guests may use a nearby health club free of charge.
Transportation: Suburban Taxi from O'Hare $17

DRURY INN
600 N Martingale Rd
Schaumburg, IL 708 517-7737

Cost: Single Rate $60–$65

Features: Restaurant and lounge near hotel. Hotel guests may use a nearby health club free of charge.

Transportation: Suburban Taxi from O'Hare $12

EMBASSY SUITES
1445 Lake Cook Rd   708 945-4500
Deerfield, IL   800 EMBASSY

Cost: Single Rate $75–$125

Features: Restaurant, lounge, health club, indoor pool.

Transportation: Suburban Taxi from O'Hare $18, Airport Express $13.75

EMBASSY SUITES
1939 N Meacham Rd   708 397-1313
Schaumburg, IL   800 EMBASSY

Cost: Single Rate $79–$135

Features: Restaurant, lounge, health club, indoor pool.

Transportation: Suburban Taxi from O'Hare $15

HILTON GARDEN INN
900 W Lake Cook Rd   708 215-8883
Buffalo Grove, IL   800 HILTONS

Cost: Single Rate $74–$84

Features: Restaurant, health club, indoor pool. Lounge near hotel.

Transportation: Courtesy van from O'Hare

HILTON & TOWERS NORTHSHORE
9599 Skokie Blvd   708 679-7000
Skokie, IL   800 HILTONS

Cost: Single Rate $89–$115
Features: Restaurant, lounge, health club, indoor pool.
Transportation: Suburban Taxi from O'Hare $18, Airport Express $13.75

HILTON SUITES
10 Drury Ln   708 941-0100
Oakbrook Terrace, IL   800 HILTONS

Cost: Single $99–$139
Features: Restaurant, lounge, health club, indoor pool.
Transportation: Suburban Taxi from O'Hare $17

HOLIDAY INN
1250 Roosevelt Rd   708 629-6000
Glen Ellyn, IL   800 HOLIDAY

Cost: Single Rate $52
Features: Restaurant, lounge. No health club or pool.
Transportation: Suburban Taxi from O'Hare $17

HOLIDAY INN
1550 N Roselle Rd   708 310-0500
Schaumburg, IL   800 HOLIDAY

Cost: Single Rate $75–$95
Features: Restaurant, lounge, 24 hr convenience store on hotel premises, health club, outdoor pool.
Transportation: Courtesy van from O'Hare

HOLIDAY INN EXPRESS
3031 Finley Rd   708 810-9500
Downers Grove, IL   800 HOLIDAY

Cost: Single Rate $56–$77
Features: Restaurant and lounge near hotel. No health club or pool.
Transportation: Suburban Taxi from O'Hare $20

HOMEWOOD SUITES
815 E American Ln   708 605-0400
Schaumburg, IL   800 225-5466

Cost: Single $65–$89
Features: Restaurant and lounge near hotel. Health club, outdoor pool.
Transportation: Suburban Taxi from O'Hare $12

HOWARD JOHNSON
9333 Skokie Blvd   708 679-4200
Skokie, IL   800 IGOHOJO

Cost: Single Rate $76–$110
Features: Restaurant, lounge, health club, indoor pool.
Transportation: Suburban Taxi from O'Hare $18, Airport Express $13.75

HYATT REGENCY
1909 Spring Rd   708 573-1234
Oak Brook, IL   800 233-1234

Cost: Single Rate $140–$160
Features: Restaurant, lounge, health club, indoor pool.
Transportation: Suburban Taxi from O'Hare $17

INDIAN LAKES RESORT
250 W Schick Rd   708 529-0200
Bloomingdale, IL   800 334-3417

Cost: Single Rate $115–125

Features: Restaurant, lounge, health club, indoor pool.
Transportation: Suburban Taxi from O'Hare $18

LA QUINTA INN
1415 W Dundee Rd   708 253-8777
Arlington Heights, IL   800 531-5900

Cost: Single Rate $60
Features: Restaurant, lounge and health club near hotel. Outdoor pool.
Transportation: Suburban Taxi from O'Hare $15

LA QUINTA INN
1 S 666 Midwest Rd   708 495-4600
Oakbrook Terrace, IL   800 531-5900

Cost: Single Rate $51–58
Features: 24 hour restaurant, lounge, and health club near hotel. Outdoor pool.
Transportation: Suburban Taxi from O'Hare $17

MARRIOTT SUITES
2 Parkway N Ctr   708 405-9666
Deerfield, IL   800 228-9290

Cost: Single Rate $125
Features: Restaurant, lounge, health club, indoor pool.
Transportation: Suburban Taxi from O'Hare $18, Airport Express $13.75

OAK BROOK HILLS HOTEL AND RESORT
3500 Midwest Rd   708 850-5555
Oakbrook, IL   800 445-3315

Cost: Single Rate $150–$170

Features: Restaurant, lounge, health club, indoor pool.
Transportation: Suburban Taxi from O'Hare $17

QUALITY HOTEL
920 E Northwest Hwy 708 359-6900
Palatine, IL 800 221-2222

Cost: Single Rate $35–$69
Features: Restaurant, lounge, health club, indoor pool.
Transportation: Suburban Taxi from O'Hare $19

RADISSON HOTEL ARLINGTON HEIGHTS
75 W Algonquin Rd 708 364-7600
Arlington Heights, IL 800 333-3333

Cost: Single Rate $49–$92
Features: Restaurant, lounge, health club, indoor pool.
Transportation: Suburban Taxi from O'Hare $15

RADISSON SUITE HOTEL
2111 Butterfield Rd 708 971-2000
Downers Grove, IL 800 333-3333

Cost: Single Rate $109
Features: Restaurant, lounge, health club, indoor pool.
Transportation: Suburban Taxi from O'Hare $20

RED ROOF INN
2500 Hassell Rd 708 885-7877
Hoffman Estates, IL 800 THE ROOF

Cost: Single Rate $31

Features: Restaurant and lounge near hotel. No health club or pool.
Transportation: Suburban Taxi from O'Hare $22

RESIDENCE INN BY MARRIOTT
2001 S Highland Av 708 629-7800
Lombard, IL 800 331-3131

Cost: Single Rate $69–$109
Features: No restaurant or lounge. Outdoor pool. For a nominal fee hotel guests may use a health club near the hotel.
Transportation: Suburban Taxi from O'Hare $17

Hotels in Downtown Chicago (Approximately 19 Miles from O'Hare)

ALLERTON HOTEL
701 N Michigan Av
Chicago, IL 312 440-1500

Cost: Single Rate $99–$119
Features: Restaurant and lounge. No health club or pool.
Transportation: Chicago Taxi from O'Hare $25, Shared Taxi $15, Airport Express $13, Subway $1.50

BARCLAY CHICAGO HOTEL
166 E Superior St
Chicago, IL 312 787-6000

Cost: Single Rate $145–$195
Features: Restaurant and lounge. For a nominal fee hotel guests may use a health club and indoor pool near the hotel.

Transportation: Chicago Taxi from O'Hare $25, Shared Taxi $15, Airport Express $13, Subway $1.50

BEST WESTERN INN OF CHICAGO
162 E Ohio St   312 787-3100
Chicago, IL   800 528-1234

Cost: Single Rate $59–$200

Features: Restaurant and lounge. For a nominal fee hotel guests may use a health club and indoor pool near the hotel.

Transportation: Chicago Taxi from O'Hare $25, Shared Taxi $15, Airport Express $13, Subway $1.50

BEST WESTERN RIVER NORTH HOTEL
125 W Ohio   312 467-0800
Chicago, IL   800 528-1234

Cost: Single Rate $78–$155

Features: Restaurant, lounge, health club, indoor pool.

Transportation: Chicago Taxi from O'Hare $25, Shared Taxi $15, Airport Express $13, Subway $1.50

BISMARCK HOTEL
171 W Randolph St   312 236-0123
Chicago, IL   800 643-1500

Cost: Single Rate $85–$95

Features: Restaurant and lounge. For a nominal fee hotel guests may use a health club and indoor pool near the hotel.

Transportation: Chicago Taxi from O'Hare $25, Shared Taxi $15, Airport Express $13, Subway $1.50

BLACKSTONE HOTEL
636 S Michigan Av
Chicago, IL   312 427-4300

Cost: Single Rate $109–$150
Features: Restaurant and lounge. No health club or pool.
Transportation: Chicago Taxi from O'Hare $25, Shared Taxi $15, Airport Express $13

CLARIDGE HOTEL
1244 N Dearborn Pkwy   312 787-4980
Chicago, IL   800 245-1258

Cost: Single Rate $100–$160
Features: Restaurant and lounge. For a nominal fee hotel guests may use a health club and indoor pool near the hotel.
Transportation: Chicago Taxi from O'Hare $25, Shared Taxi $15, Airport Express $13

CONGRESS HOTEL
520 S Michigan Av   312 427-3800
Chicago, IL   800 635-1666

Cost: Single Rate $115–$155
Features: Restaurant and lounge. For a nominal fee hotel guests may use a health club and indoor pool near the hotel.
Transportation: Chicago Taxi from O'Hare $25, Shared Taxi $15, Airport Express $13

COURTYARD BY MARRIOTT
30 E Hubbard St   312 329-2500
Chicago, IL   800 321-2211

Cost: Single Rate $129

Features: Restaurant, lounge, health club, indoor pool.

Transportation: Chicago Taxi from O'Hare $25, Shared Taxi $15, Airport Express $13, Subway $1.50

DAYS INN – Chicago Lake Shore
644 N Lake Shore Dr   312 943-9200
Chicago, IL   800 325-2525

Cost: Single Rate $69–$139

Features: Restaurant, lounge, health club, outdoor pool.

Transportation: Chicago Taxi from O'Hare $25, Shared Taxi $15, Airport Express $13

THE DRAKE
140 E Walton Pl   312 787-2200
Chicago, IL   800 55DRAKE

Cost: Single Rate $185–$205

Features: Restaurant, lounge, 24 hr room service, health club. No pool.

Transportation: Chicago Taxi from O'Hare $25, Shared Taxi $15, Airport Express $13

EMBASSY SUITES
600 N State St   312 943-3800
Chicago, IL   800 EMBASSY

Cost: Single Rate $139–$249

Features: Restaurant, lounge, health club, indoor pool.

Transportation: Chicago Taxi from O'Hare $25, Shared Taxi $15, Airport Express $13, Subway $1.50

EXECUTIVE PLAZA CLARION
71 E Wacker Dr 312 346-7100
Chicago, IL 800 221-2222

Cost: Single Rate $155–$175
Features: Restaurant, lounge, health club. No pool.
Transportation: Chicago Taxi from O'Hare $25, Shared Taxi $15, Airport Express $13, Subway $1.50

FAIRMONT HOTEL
200 N Columbus Dr 312 565-8000
Chicago, IL 800 562-1003

Cost: Single Rate $185–$205
Features: Restaurant, lounge. For a nominal fee hotel guests may use a health club and indoor pool near the hotel.
Transportation: Chicago Taxi from O'Hare $25, Shared Taxi $15, Airport Express $13

FORUM HOTEL
505 N Michigan Av 312 944-0055
Chicago, IL 800 628-2112

Cost: Single Rate $135–$165
Features: Restaurant, lounge. For a nominal fee hotel guests may use a health club and indoor pool near the hotel.
Transportation: Chicago Taxi from O'Hare $25, Shared Taxi $15, Airport Express $13

FOUR SEASONS HOTEL
120 E Delaware Pl 312 280-8800
Chicago, IL 800 628-2112

Cost: Single Rate $210–$240

Features: Restaurant, lounge, 24 hr room service, health club, indoor pool.

Transportation: Chicago Taxi from O'Hare $25, Shared Taxi $15, Airport Express $13

GUEST QUARTERS SUITE HOTEL
198 E Delaware Pl	312 644-1100
Chicago, IL	800 424-2900

Cost: Single Rate $149–$195

Features: Restaurant, lounge, health club, indoor pool.

Transportation: Chicago Taxi from O'Hare $25, Shared Taxi $15, Airport Express $13

HILTON & TOWERS CHICAGO
720 S Michigan Av	312 922-4400
Chicago, IL	800 HILTONS

Cost: Single Rate $99–$249

Features: Restaurant, lounge, 24 hr room service, health club, indoor pool.

Transportation: Chicago Taxi from O'Hare $25, Shared Taxi $15, Airport Express $13

HOLIDAY INN CITY CENTRE
300 E Ohio St	312 787-6100
Chicago, IL	800 HOLIDAY

Cost: Single Rate $99–$180

Features: Restaurant, lounge, health club, indoor pool.

Transportation: Chicago Taxi from O'Hare $25, Shared Taxi $15, Airport Express $13

HOLIDAY INN MART PLAZA
350 N Orleans St	312 836-5000
Chicago, IL	800 HOLIDAY

Cost: Single Rate $124–$137

Features: Restaurant, lounge, health club, indoor pool.

Transportation: Chicago Taxi from O'Hare $25, Shared Taxi $15, Airport Express $13

HOJO INN
720 N LaSalle St 312 664-8100
Chicago, IL 800 IGOHOJO

Cost: Single Rate $54–$60

Features: Restaurant, lounge near hotel. No health club or pool.

Transportation: Chicago Taxi from O'Hare $25, Shared Taxi $15, Airport Express $13

PARK HYATT
800 N Michigan Av 312 280-2222
Chicago, IL 800 233-1234

Cost: Single Rate $225–$300

Features: Restaurant, lounge, 24 hr room service. For a nominal fee hotel guests may use a health club and indoor pool near the hotel.

Transportation: Chicago Taxi from O'Hare $25, Shared Taxi $15, Airport Express $13, Subway $1.50

HYATT ON PRINTER'S ROW
500 S Dearborn St 312 986-1234
Chicago, IL 800 233-1234

Cost: Single Rate $175

Features: Restaurant, lounge. For a nominal fee hotel guests may use a health club and indoor pool near the hotel.

Transportation: Chicago Taxi from O'Hare $25, Shared Taxi $15, Airport Express $13, Subway $1.50

HYATT REGENCY CHICAGO
151 E Wacker Dr   312 565-1234
Chicago, IL   800 233-1234

Cost: Single Rate $200–$225
Features: Restaurant, lounge, 24 hr room service. For a nominal fee hotel guests may use a health club and indoor pool near the hotel.
Transportation: Chicago Taxi from O'Hare $25, Shared Taxi $15, Airport Express $13

HYATT REGENCY SUITES
676 N Michigan Av   312 337-1234
Chicago, IL   800 233-1234

Cost: Single Rate $215–$245
Features: Restaurant, lounge, 24 hr room service, health club, indoor pool.
Transportation: Chicago Taxi from O'Hare $25, Shared Taxi $15, Airport Express $13

INN AT UNIVERSITY VILLAGE
625 S Ashland Av   312 234-7200
Chicago, IL   800 662-5233

Cost: Single Rate $70–$150
Features: Restaurant and lounge. Health club on premises and hotel guests may pay a nominal fee for use of University of Illinois health club facilities, bowling alley and indoor pool.
Transportation: Chicago Taxi from O'Hare $25, Shared Taxi $15, Airport Express $13

INTER-CONTINENTAL
505 N Michigan Av   312 944-4100
Chicago, IL   800 628-2468

Cost: Single Rate $190–$250
Features: Restaurant, lounge, health club, indoor pool.
Transportation: Chicago Taxi from O'Hare $25, Shared Taxi $15, Airport Express $13

KNICKERBOCKER HOTEL
163 E Walton Pl
Chicago, IL   312 751-8100

Cost: Single Rate $135–$195
Features: Restaurant, lounge. For a nominal fee hotel guests may use a health club and indoor pool near the hotel.
Transportation: Chicago Taxi from O'Hare $25, Shared Taxi $15, Airport Express $13

LA SALLE CLUB HOTEL
440 S La Salle St
Chicago, IL   312 663-8910

Cost: Single Rate $150–$350
Features: Restaurant, lounge, health club, indoor pool.
Transportation: Chicago Taxi from O'Hare $25, Shared Taxi $15, Airport Express $13, Subway $1.50

LE MERIDIEN
21 E Bellevue Pl
Chicago, IL   312 266-2100

Cost: Single Rate $195–$270
Features: Restaurant, lounge, health club. No pool.

Transportation: Chicago Taxi from O'Hare $25, Shared Taxi $15, Airport Express $13

LENOX HOUSE
616 N Rush St
Chicago, IL   312 337-1000

Cost: Single Rate $109–$164
Features: Restaurant, lounge. No health club or pool.
Transportation: Chicago Taxi from O'Hare $25, Shared Taxi $15, Airport Express $13, Subway $1.50

MARRIOTT
540 N Michigan Ave   312 836-0100
Chicago, IL   800 228-9290

Cost: Single Rate $119–$209
Features: Restaurant, lounge, health club, indoor pool.
Transportation: Chicago Taxi from O'Hare $25, Shared Taxi $15, Airport Express $13

MIDLAND HOTEL
172 W Adams St   312 332-1200
Chicago, IL   800 621-2360

Cost: Single Rate $150–$220
Features: Restaurant, lounge. Health club and indoor pool near hotel.
Transportation: Chicago Taxi from O'Hare $25, Shared Taxi $15, Airport Express $13, Subway $1.50

NIKKO
320 N Dearborn St   312 744-1900
Chicago, IL   800 645-5687

Cost: Single Rate $175–$215
Features: Restaurant, lounge, health club. No pool.
Transportation: Chicago Taxi from O'Hare $25, Shared Taxi $15, Airport Express $13

OHIO HOUSE
600 N LaSalle St
Chicago, IL   312 943-6000

Cost: Single Rate $53–$70
Features: Restaurant, lounge near hotel. No health club or pool.
Transportation: Chicago Taxi from O'Hare $25, Shared Taxi $15, Airport Express $13

OMNI AMBASSADOR EAST HOTEL
1301 N State Pkwy
Chicago, IL   312 787-7200

Cost: Single Rate $185–$195
Features: Restaurant, lounge, 24 hr room service. No health club or pool.
Transportation: Chicago Taxi from O'Hare $25, Shared Taxi $15, Airport Express $13

OXFORD HOUSE
225 N Wabash Av   312 346-6585
Chicago, IL   800 344-4111

Cost: Single Rate $75–$190
Features: Restaurant, lounge. No health club or pool.
Transportation: Chicago Taxi from O'Hare $25, Shared Taxi $15, Airport Express $13, Subway $1.50

PALMER HOUSE
17 E Monroe St   312 726-7500
Chicago, IL   800 HILTONS

Cost: Single Rate $129–$169
Features: Restaurant, lounge, health club, indoor pool.
Transportation: Chicago Taxi from O'Hare $25, Shared Taxi $15, Airport Express $13, Subway $1.50

RADISSON PLAZA AMBASSADOR WEST
1300 N State Pkwy   312 787-7900
Chicago, IL   800 333-3333

Cost: Single Rate $99–$215
Features: Restaurant, lounge. No health club or pool.
Transportation: Chicago Taxi from O'Hare $25, Shared Taxi $15, Airport Express $13

RALPHAEL HOTEL
201 E Delaware Pl
Chicago, IL   312 943-5000

Cost: Single Rate $110
Features: Restaurant, lounge. For a nominal fee hotel guests may use a health club and indoor pool near the hotel.
Transportation: Chicago Taxi from O'Hare $25, Shared Taxi $15, Airport Express $13

RESIDENCE INN BY MARRIOTT
201 E Walton St   312 943-9800
Chicago, IL   800 331-3131

Cost: Single Rate $139–$189
Features: Health club and indoor pool. Restaurant and lounge near the hotel.
Transportation: Chicago Taxi from O'Hare $25, Shared Taxi $15, Airport Express $13

RICHMONT HOTEL
163 E Ontario St 312 787-3580
Chicago, IL 800 621-8055

Cost: Single Rate $105–$135

Features: Restaurant and lounge. No health club or pool.

Transportation: Chicago Taxi from O'Hare $25, Shared Taxi $15, Airport Express $13

RITZ CARLTON HOTEL
160 E Pearson St 312 266-1000
Chicago, IL 800 332-3422

Cost: Single Rate $210–$240

Features: Restaurant, lounge, health club, indoor pool.

Transportation: Chicago Taxi from O'Hare $25, Shared Taxi $15, Airport Express $13

SHERATON CHICAGO HOTEL & TOWERS
301 E North Water St 312 464-1000
Chicago, IL 800 325-3535

Cost: Single Rate $180–$215

Features: Restaurant, lounge, 24 hr room service, health club, indoor pool.

Transportation: Chicago Taxi from O'Hare $25, Shared Taxi $15, Airport Express $13

SHERATON PLAZA HOTEL
160 E Huron St 312 787-2900
Chicago, IL 800 325-3535

Cost: Single Rate $145–$175

Features: Restaurant, lounge, outdoor pool. No health club.

Transportation: Chicago Taxi from O'Hare $25, Shared Taxi $15, Airport Express $13

STOUFFER RIVIERE HOTEL
One W Wacker Dr 312 372-7200
Chicago, IL 800 HOTELS1

Cost: Single Rate $205–$300

Features: Restaurant, lounge, health club, indoor pool.

Transportation: Chicago Taxi from O'Hare $25, Shared Taxi $15, Airport Express $13, Subway $1.50

SWISSOTEL
323 E Wacker Dr 312 565-0565
Chicago, IL 800 654-7262

Cost: Single Rate $175–$220

Features: Restaurant, lounge, health club, indoor pool.

Transportation: Chicago Taxi from O'Hare $25, Shared Taxi $15, Airport Express $13

TALBOTT HOTEL
20 E Delaware Pl 312 943-0161
Chicago, IL 800 621-8506

Cost: Single Rate $155–$175

Features: Restaurant, lounge. No health club or pool.

Transportation: Chicago Taxi from O'Hare $25, Shared Taxi $15, Airport Express $13

TREMONT HOTEL
100 E Chestnut St 312 751-1900
Chicago, IL 800 621-8133

Cost: Single Rate $170–$205

Features: Restaurant, lounge. For a nominal fee hotel guests may use a health club and indoor pool near the hotel.

Transportation: Chicago Taxi from O'Hare $25, Shared Taxi $15, Airport Express $13

WESTIN HOTEL
909 N Michigan Av
Chicago, IL   312 943-7200

Cost: Single Rate $165–$195

Features: Restaurant, lounge, 24 hr room service, health club. No pool.

Transportation: Chicago Taxi from O'Hare $25, Shared Taxi $15, Airport Express $13

RESTAURANTS

Hungry? Don't be fooled by self-service restaurants at O'Hare; there's more to local cuisine than the airport's ubiquitous hot dogs, pretzels and frozen yoghurt. Not satisfied with ordinary pizza, Chicagoans created a nationwide sensation when they invented deep dish pizza. Hearty eaters here also invented the Hostess Twinkie, Cracker Jack, M & M's, Dove ice cream bars and the Weber Grill. And don't forget that the real Sara Lee grew up here!

Finding great food is made easy by Chicago's diverse population, people who are proud to prepare and serve specialty dishes to hungry customers. You'll find a **Polish buffet,** a **rustic retreat** in the woods, **Chicago's best ribs,** and even **flaming food** just a short distance from O'Hare. Restaurants listed in **STRANDED AT O'HARE** are distinct and yet they have two things in common: Each restaurant has been favorably reviewed by the local media and each restaurant is located within a few miles of O'Hare.

Restaurants By Cuisine

American: Denny's, Bennigan's, Knicker's, Sally's Waffle Shoppe

Chinese: The Bird

Continental: Cafe Parisien, Fountain Blue, Horwath's, Nielsen's, Plentywood Farms

French: Cafe de Paris

Italian: Armand's, Basta Pasta, Cafe Fettucini, Carlucci, Giannotti's, Giovanni's, Pasta Vino, Portico, Ristorante Agostino, Ristorante Italia, Romano's, Slicker Sam's, Trattoria Veneta, Villa, Vince's

Korean: Kimchy Cabana

Mexican: Don Juan's, Maria's

Middle Eastern: Sayat Nova

Pizza: Giordano's, Nancy's, Sergio's Pub

Polish: Red Apple

Ribs: Carson's, Giovanni's, Rog's Turtle Inn, Russell's Barbecue

Russian: Rasputin, White Nights

Seafood: Benchmark, Black Ram, Cafe La Cave, Corgi's, Crabs & Things, Kona Kai, Nick's Fishmarket, Red Lobster, Rosewood, Walter's

Steak: Benchmark, Black Ram, Cafe La Cave, Corgi's, Giannotti's, Morton's, Nick's Fishmarket, Pasta Vino, Rog's Turtle Inn, Rosewood, Walter's

Restaurants in the Airport

Each terminal has its own assortment of yoghurt bars, hot dog stands, popcorn wagons and sandwich shops. The bill of fare in the **Restaurant Rotunda** includes pizza, deli food, fresh salads and made to order breakfasts. In the **O'Hare Hilton,** across from Terminal #2, you'll find an Italian restaurant, a sports bar and the Gaslight Club.

Restaurants near O'Hare

ARMAND'S
7400 W Grand Av
Elmwood Park, IL   708 456-5200

Type: Italian
Hours: Lunch Mon-Fri, Dinner Daily
Transportation: Any Taxi from O'Hare $17
Price Range: Moderate

BASTA PASTA
6733 N Olmstead Av
Chicago, IL   312 763-1096

Type: Italian
Hours: Lunch and Dinner Tues-Sun
Transportation: Chicago Taxi from O'Hare $8
Price Range: Moderate

BENCHMARK
6100 N River Rd (Westin Hotel)
Rosemont, IL   708 698-6000

Type: Steak and Seafood
Hours: Dinner Daily
Transportation: Any taxi from O'Hare $5, Subway $1.50
Price Range: Moderate

BENNIGAN'S
8420 W Bryn Mawr Av
Chicago, IL   312 380-1010

Type: American
Hours: Lunch and Dinner Daily, Late Dining Hours
Transportation: Chicago Taxi from O'Hare $7, Subway $1.50
Price Range: Inexpensive

THE BIRD
119 N 25th Av
Melrose Park, IL   708 681-0414

Type: Chinese
Hours: Dinner Wed-Sat
Transportation: Suburban Taxi from O'Hare $15
Price Range: Moderate

BLACK RAM
1414 Oakton St
Des Plaines, IL   708 824-1227

Type: Steak and Seafood
Hours: Lunch Mon-Fri, Dinner Daily
Transportation: Any Taxi from O'Hare $12
Price Range: Moderate

CAFE DE PARIS
5550 N River Rd (Hotel Sofitel)
Rosemont, IL   708 678-4488

Type: French
Hours: Dinner Mon-Sat
Transportation: Any Taxi from O'Hare $5, Subway $1.50
Price Range: Expensive

CAFE LA CAVE
2777 Mannheim Rd
Des Plaines, IL   708 827-7818

Type: Steak and Seafood
Hours: Lunch Mon-Fri, Dinner Daily, Late Dining Hours.
Transportation: Any Taxi from O'Hare $12
Price Range: Expensive

CAFE FETTUCINI
4701 N Cumberland Av
Norridge, IL   708 452-6400

Type: Italian
Hours: Dinner Daily, Late Dining Hours
Transportation: Any Taxi from O'Hare $12
Price Range: Moderate

CAFE PARISIEN
696 W North Av
Elmhurst, IL   708 279-3310

Type: Continental
Hours: Lunch Mon-Fri, Dinner Mon-Sat
Transportation: Suburban Taxi from O'Hare $17
Price Range: Moderate

CARLUCCI
6111 River Rd
Rosemont, IL   708 518-0990

Type: Italian
Hours: Lunch Mon-Fri, Dinner Mon-Sat, Late Dining Hours
Transportation: Any Taxi from O'Hare $8, Subway $1.50
Price Range: Expensive

CARSON'S RIBS
5050 N Harlem Av
Harwood Heights, IL   708 867-4200

Type: Ribs
Hours: Lunch and Dinner Daily, Late Dining Hours
Transportation: Any Taxi from O'Hare $12
Price Range: Moderate

CORGI'S
5440 N River Rd (Holiday Inn)
Rosemont, IL   708 671-6350

Type: Steak and Seafood
Hours: Dinner Daily
Transportation: Any Taxi from O'Hare $5, Subway $1.50
Price Range: Moderate

CRABS & THINGS
1249 S Elmhurst Rd
Des Plaines, IL   708 437-1595

Type: Seafood
Hours: Lunch Mon-Fri, Dinner Daily, Late Dining Hours

Transportation: Any Taxi from O'Hare $12
Price Range: Moderate

DENNY'S
8225 W Higgins Rd
Chicago, IL   312 399-1190

Type: American
Hours: Breakfast, Lunch and Dinner Daily, Open 24 Hours
Transportation: Chicago Taxi from O'Hare $5, Subway $1.50
Price Range: Inexpensive

DON JUAN'S
6730 N Northwest Hwy
Chicago, IL   312 775-6438

Type: Mexican
Hours: Lunch and Dinner Daily
Transportation: Chicago Taxi from O'Hare $11
Price Range: Moderate

FOUNTAIN BLUE
2300 Mannheim Rd
Des Plaines, IL   708 298-3636

Type: Continental
Hours: Lunch Mon-Fri, Dinner Daily
Transportation: Any Taxi from O'Hare $12
Price Range: Moderate

GIANNOTTI'S
8422 W Lawrence Av
Norridge, IL   708 453-1616

Type: Italian and Steak
Hours: Lunch Mon-Fri, Dinner Daily

Transportation: Any Taxi from O'Hare $12
Price Range: Moderate

GIORDANO'S
9415 W Higgins Rd
Rosemont, IL   708 292-2600

Type: Pizza
Hours: Lunch and Dinner Daily
Transportation: Any Taxi from O'Hare $8
Price Range: Inexpensive

GIOVANNI'S
600 E Central Rd
Des Plaines, IL   708 298-3311

Type: Italian and Ribs
Hours: Lunch on Weekends, Dinner Daily
Transportation: Any Taxi from O'Hare $12
Price Range: Moderate

HORWATH'S
1850 Harlem Av
Elmwood Park, IL   708 453-0413

Type: Continental
Hours: Lunch and Dinner Daily, Late Dining Hours
Transportation: Any Taxi from O'Hare $17
Price Range: Moderate

KIMCHY CABANA
9020 N Greenwood Rd
Des Plaines, IL   708 827-9021

Type: Korean
Hours: Lunch and Dinner Tues-Sun
Transportation: Any Taxi from O'Hare $12
Price Range: Inexpensive

KNICKER'S
1050 E Oakton St
Des Plaines, IL   708 299-0011

Type: American
Hours: Dinner Daily, Late Dining Hours
Transportation: Any Taxi from O'Hare $12
Price Range: Moderate

KONA KAI
8535 W Higgins (Marriott)
Chicago, IL   312 693-4444

Type: Seafood
Hours: Dinner Daily
Transportation: Chicago Taxi from O'Hare $5,
   Subway $1.50
Price Range: Moderate

MARIA'S
9440 Foster Ave
Chicago, IL   312 992-2288

Type: Mexican
Hours: Lunch Sun-Fri, Dinner Daily, Late Dining
   Hours
Transportation: Chicago Taxi from O'Hare $5
Price Range: Inexpensive

MORTON'S
9525 W Bryn Mawr Av
Rosemont, IL   708 678-5155

Type: Steak
Hours: Lunch Mon-Fri, Dinner Daily
Transportation: Any Taxi from O'Hare $8
Price Range: Expensive

NANCY'S
8706 W Golf Rd
Des Plaines, IL 708 824-8183

Type: Pizza
Hours: Dinner Daily, Late Dining Hours
Transportation: Any Taxi from O'Hare $12
Price Range: Inexpensive

NICK'S FISHMARKET
10275 W Higgins Rd
Rosemont, IL 708 298-8200

Type: Steak and Seafood
Hours: Dinner Daily, Late Dining Hours
Transportation: Any Taxi from O'Hare $8
Price Range: Expensive

NIELSEN'S
7330 W North Av
Elmwood Park, IL 708 453-9200

Type: Continental, flaming tableside cooking
Hours: Lunch Daily, Dinner Tues-Sun, Late Dining Hours
Transportation: Any Taxi from O'Hare $17
Price Range: Moderate

PASTA VINO
4200 River Rd
Schiller Park, IL 708 678-2000

Type: Italian and Steak
Hours: Lunch Mon-Fri, Dinner Daily, Late Dining Hours
Transportation: Suburban Taxi from O'Hare $9
Price Range: Moderate

PLENTYWOOD FARMS
130 S Church Rd
Bensenville, IL 708 860-4570

Type: Continental
Hours: Lunch Daily, Dinner Tues-Sun
Transportation: Suburban Taxi from O'Hare $17
Price Range: Moderate

PORTICO
6600 N Mannheim (Ramada Hotel)
Rosemont, IL 708 827-5131

Type: Italian
Hours: Dinner Daily
Transportation: Any Taxi from O'Hare $5
Price Range: Moderate

RASPUTIN
1730 S Elmhurst Rd
Des Plaines, IL 708 956-1992

Type: Russian
Hours: Lunch and Dinner Tues-Sun
Transportation: Any Taxi from O'Hare $12
Price Range: Moderate

RED APPLE
6474 N Milwaukee Av
Chicago, IL 312 763-3407

Type: Polish Buffet
Hours: Lunch and Dinner Daily, Late Dining Hours
Transportation: Chicago Taxi from O'Hare $11
Price Range: Inexpensive

RED LOBSTER
4401 Cumberland Ave
Norridge, IL 708 456-7966

Type: Seafood
Hours: Lunch and Dinner Daily
Transportation: Any Taxi from O'Hare $12
Price Range: Moderate

RISTORANTE AGOSTINO
2817 N Harlem Av
Chicago, IL   312 745-6464

Type: Italian
Hours: Dinner Tues-Sun
Transportation: Chicago Taxi from O'Hare $17
Price Range: Moderate

RISTORANTE ITALIA
2631 N Harlem Av
Chicago, IL   312 889-5008

Type: Italian
Hours: Dinner Tues-Sun, Late Dining Hours
Transportation: Chicago Taxi from O'Hare $17
Price Range: Moderate

ROG'S TURTLE INN
9800 Irving Park Rd
Schiller Park, IL   708 678-1974

Type: Steak and Ribs
Hours: Lunch and Dinner Daily, Late Dining Hours
Transportation: Suburban Taxi from O'Hare $9
Price Range: Moderate

ROMANO'S
1396 Oakton St
Des Plaines, IL   708 827-5571

Type: Italian

Hours: Lunch Tues-Fri and Sunday, Dinner
   Tues-Sun
Transportation: Any Taxi from O'Hare $12
Price Range: Moderate

ROSEWOOD
9421 W Higgins Rd
Rosemont, IL   708 696-9494

Type: Steak and Seafood
Hours: Lunch Mon-Fri, Dinner Mon-Sat, Late
   Dining Hours
Transportation: Any Taxi from O'Hare $8
Price Range: Moderate

RUSSELL'S BARBECUE
1621 Thatcher Rd
Elmwood Park, IL   708 453-7065

Type: Ribs, Chicken, BBQ
Hours: Lunch and Dinner Daily, Late Dining Hours
Transportation: Any Taxi from O'Hare $17
Price Range: Inexpensive

SALLY'S WAFFLE SHOPPE
5454 N Harlem Av
Chicago, IL   312 631-8966

Type: American
Hours: Breakfast, Lunch and Dinner Daily, Late
   Dining Hours, Open 24 Hours on Weekends
Transportation: Chicago Taxi from O'Hare $8,
   Subway $1.50
Price Range: Inexpensive

SAYAT NOVA
20 W Golf Rd
Des Plaines, IL   708 296-1776

Type: Middle Eastern
Hours: Lunch Tues-Fri, Dinner Tues-Sun, Late Dining Hours
Transportation: Any Taxi from O'Hare $12
Price Range: Moderate

SERGIO'S PUB
9800 W Lawrence Av
Schiller Park, IL   708 678-7096

Type: Pizza
Hours: Lunch and Dinner Mon-Sat, Late Dining Hours
Transportation: Suburban Taxi from O'Hare $9
Price Range: Inexpensive

SLICKER SAM'S
1911 Rice
Melrose Park, IL   708 344-3660

Type: Italian
Hours: Lunch Tues-Sat, Dinner Tues-Sun
Transportation: Suburban Taxi from O'Hare $15
Price Range: Inexpensive

TRATTORIA VENETA
3426 N Harlem Ave
Chicago, IL   312 622-7888

Type: Italian
Hours: Dinner Wed-Mon
Transportation: Chicago Taxi from O'Hare $15
Price Range: Moderate

VILLA
7443 W Irving Park Rd
Chicago, IL   312 625-3636

Type: Italian
Hours: Dinner Daily
Transportation: Chicago Taxi from O'Hare $9
Price Range: Inexpensive

VINCE'S
4747 N Harlem Av
Harwood Heights, IL 708 867-7770

Type: Italian
Hours: Lunch and Dinner Daily, Late Dining Hours
Transportation: Any Taxi from O'Hare $12
Price Range: Moderate

WALTER'S
28 Main St
Park Ridge, IL 708 825-2240

Type: Steak and Seafood
Hours: Lunch Tues-Fri, Dinner Tues-Sat
Transportation: Any Taxi from O'Hare $12
Price Range: Moderate

TRANSPORTATION

LONG DISTANCE TRANSPORTATION

Your flight has been cancelled. You can't get to your meeting and you're not happy. If we tell you how you can reach your final destination within the next few hours will you be happy? Okay. Start smiling.

Other Airports

While O'Hare is one of the most famous airports in the world it isn't the only airport in the area. Less glamorous and more gritty than O'Hare is **Midway Airport** (312) 767-0500 located in a working class neighborhood on Chicago's Southwest side. TWA, USAir, Northwest, Southwest, and several smaller airlines fly from **Midway** to major U.S. cities. Chicago's third airport, tiny **Meigs Field** (312) 744-4787 in downtown Chicago, is served by Trans World Express (312) 427-1120 and United Express (312)

922-9010 as well as by private aircraft. Uncongested **General Mitchell International Airport** is only 90 miles from O'Hare. American, Continental, Delta, Northwest, United, Midwest Express and other airlines fly non-stop to more than 40 destinations from Milwaukee's **General Mitchell International Airport.**

Trains

Chicago is a major hub for **Amtrak's** nationwide rail service. Trains with names like The Desert Wind, The Texas Eagle, The Empire Builder and The City of New Orleans begin their cross country journeys from downtown Chicago.

Bear in mind that Chicago has four train stations each within a few blocks of each other; **Amtrak** departs from **Union Station.** To reach **Union Station** take the subway from O'Hare to Clinton St and walk two blocks North to Jackson St or take any waiting taxi directly to the station's Amtrak entrance at 210 S Canal St (full fare $25, shared ride $15). Call **Amtrak** (800) 872-7245 or (312) 558-1075 for departure information.

Car Rental

If your flight is 600 miles or less (40% of flights from O'Hare are, you know), you could drive to your destination in less than 10 hours. The following **car rental agencies** operate at O'Hare:

Airways   708 671-7070

Alamo	708 671-7662
Avis	312 694-5600
Budget	312 686-6800
Dollar	312 694-2200
Hertz	312 686-7272
National	312 694-4640
Thrifty	708 928-2000

Greyhound

A bus may not be your preferred mode of transportation but it might just get you to your destination on time. Chicago's mammoth **Greyhound** station, complete with fast food restaurants and cavernous waiting room, was recently razed to make way for an office building. The new terminal, located West of the Loop at 630 W Harrison, is just large enough to accommodate several dozen bolted down chairs and a food concession. What the station lost in size it gained in security. No one is allowed in the building without a valid ticket and loiters are asked to leave the station. For departure information call **Greyhound** at (312) 781-2900.

To reach the **Greyhound** Station take any waiting taxi for $25 (Shared Ride $15) or take the subway from Terminal #4 to Clinton St and walk one block South to Harrison then one block West on Harrison to Jefferson.

If you are travelling to Minneapolis, Milwaukee or Des Moines you can depart from a small **Greyhound** station near O'Hare; call (312) 693-2474.

LOCAL TRANSPORTATION

To Downtown Chicago

The **cab fare from O'Hare to downtown Chicago** is currently around $25. If you don't mind waiting a few minutes and sharing a cab with other passengers, your fare will be discounted to $15. Just tell the dispatcher that you want a "Shared Ride".

Continental Air Transport/Airport Express minivans (312) 454-7800 take passengers from the departure level of each terminal to downtown Chicago and near north side hotels from 6am-11:30pm. The fare is $13.

The **subway** sails past lines of slow moving vehicles on its way to Chicago's Loop and it costs just $1.50. Taking the subway is especially advisable during rush hour when the Kennedy Expressway is choked with traffic. Subway trains leave the station beneath Terminal #4 every few minutes.

To the Suburbs

Before you grab a taxi at O'Hare you should know that cab rates to suburban addresses can be expensive if you choose the wrong type of cab. Taxis licensed by the City of Chicago, the cabs you see waiting in line at O'Hare taxi stands, charge up to 50% more than the metered rate for trips to many suburbs.

To avoid the extra cost call a suburban cab company when you arrive. Although drivers of suburban cabs can't cruise the airport looking for fares they are allowed into the airport in response to a request by a passenger.

If you hop into a cab that is waiting at the curb at O'Hare expect to pay the **metered rate plus 50% to these suburbs:** Addison, Arlington Heights, Bensenville, Bloomingdale, Buffalo Grove, Deerfield, Downers Grove, Elk Grove Village, Elmhurst, Franklin Park, Glen Ellyn, Glenview, Hillside, Hoffman Estates, Itasca, La Grange, Lombard, Maywood, Melrose Park, Morton Grove, Mt. Prospect, Northbrook, Oak Brook, Oak Brook Terrace, Palatine, Prospect Heights, Rolling Meadows, Schaumburg, Schiller Park, Skokie, Stone Park, Villa Park, Westchester and Wood Dale.

There is **no surcharge for trips to these destinations:** Cicero, Des Plaines, Elmwood Park, Evanston, Harwood Heights, Lincolnwood, Niles, Norridge, Oak Park, Park Ridge, Rosemont, or Chicago.

Continental Air Transport/Airport Express minivans make regularly scheduled trips between 6am-11pm to several hotels in Deerfield, Evanston, Lincolnwood and Skokie. The fare is $13.75. For reservations call (800) 654-7871.

The **prearranged ride boards** near the luggage carrousels list a confusing array of taxi and limousine companies but the boards aren't of much help unless a destination can be pinpointed on the blurry maps and cross referenced on a chart. Here is some advice that will make choosing a taxi company simple. For a trip to Chicago use any waiting cab. For a trip to the suburbs avoid the 50% surcharge by using a suburban cab company. The following taxis go to all suburban destinations in this book: American Taxi (708) 255-9600; Horizon Cab (708) 678-0100; Rosemont Taxi (708) 827-0110.

To Midway Airport

Two van companies make daily pick ups from outside the Restaurant Rotunda. **C.W. Airport Service** (312) 493-2700 operates from 6:30am-11pm daily. The fare is $13. **Tri-State Coach Lines** (312) 374-7200 leaves between 6:45am-6:45pm daily; the fare is $10. Chicago based cabs charge approximately $40. The trip takes about 1 hour depending upon traffic. **Midway Airport** can also be reached by taking the new subway line. Take the subway from O'Hare to downtown Chicago and transfer at Lake St to the Midway Line.

To General Mitchell Airport

Badger Bus (414) 276-7490 makes daily trips from 9:15am-8:30pm for $13. **United Limo** (800) 833-5555 leaves daily from 7:10am-11:15pm. The fare is $14. All departures leave from outside the Restaurant Rotunda.

To Meigs Field

The taxi fare is $25, a shared taxi ride is $15.

City Tax

Unless you take the subway expect your driver to collect a Chicago tax of $1 per person each time you leave or return to the airport.

AIRLINES

Domestic Airlines Serving O'Hare:

America West	800 247-5692
American	800 433-7300
American Trans Air	800 831-9117
Continental	800 525-0280
Delta	800 221-1212
Northwest	800 225-2525
TWA	800 221-2000
United 24R 6522	800 ~~426-5561~~
USAir	800 428-4322

Airlines Serving Midway:

America West	800 247-5692
American Trans Air	800 831-9117
Delta Comair	800 354-9822

Direct	800 428-0706
Kiwi	800 538-5494
Mark	800 426-6784
Northwest	800 225-2525
Skybus	800 7SKYBUS
Skyway	800 452-2022
Southwest	800 435-9792
TWA	800 221-2000
USAir	800 428-4322

Airlines Serving Mitchell Field:

American	800 433-7300
Continental	800 525-0280
Delta	800 221-1212
Midwest Express	800 452-2022
Northwest	800 225-2525
Skyway	800 452-2022
TWA	800 221-2000
United	800 426-5561
USAir	800 428-4322

BUSINESS SERVICES

Tucked away in the basement of the **O'Hare Hilton** you'll find the **Business Center at O'Hare,** which provides a complete line of business support services – secretarial services, meeting rooms, FAX machines, court reporters, messengers, photocopy machines, computers, and shipping services (UPS and Federal Express). The **Business Center at O'Hare** is open Monday through Friday, 8am-7pm, (312) 686-0400. The **Skybird Meeting Centre** in the Restaurant Rotunda between Terminals #2 and #3 rents fully equipped meeting space for small and large groups. **Skybird** is open 7am-7pm Monday through Friday and by appointment on weekends, (312) 686-6101.

The **United States post office** offers a full range of services Monday through Friday 7am-7pm in Terminal #2, Upper Level and stamps can be purchased at any time from a self-service machine at the post office entrance. Mail boxes are located in each terminal.

If you need to make photocopies, or rent a computer, or send a FAX in the wee small hours of the morning, take any taxi to the 24 hour **Kinko's Copies** at 1720 Harlem Av in Elmwood Park (708) 453-0009; it's about 6 miles from the airport.

ENTERTAINMENT

If you're in the mood for something more exciting than a cocktail served in a plastic cup and a view of a runway you'll be pleasantly surprised by the diversity of entertainment near O'Hare. Believe it or not, there's a **Russian nightclub** at the edge of the airport where Russian is spoken as freely as English and patrons nibble caviar and quaff vodka by the bottle.

A few miles (and 800 years) from O'Hare lies a **medieval dinner theater** complete with saucy wenches who serve a six course bill of fare while jesters and minstrels amuse guests. If your taste in nightlife leans toward contemporary entertainment, check out the **Rosemont Horizon,** a concert hall that plays host to major attractions (Paul McCartney, the Grateful Dead, etc.) or see an exhibition—an RV show, camping show or crafts show—at the **Rosemont O'Hare Expo.** Both complexes are located in nearby Rosemont.

A sudden explosion of **country/western dance clubs** in the suburban area has some city slickers baffled by their popularity while others simply put on their cowboy boots and kick up their heels. Good, inexpensive food; live bands and free dance lessons are perhaps some of the reasons why country/western dance clubs have quickly gained public approval.

A day at the races always beats a day at the airport so spend some time, and some money, at one of Chicagoland's racetracks. Some of the country's finest thoroughbreds and largest purses can be found at the elegant **Arlington International Racecourse** which caps its season with the Arlington Million.

It is with some caution that we mention two more establishments. Dana Montana, a former Playboy bunny, introduced exotic male dancers to the country, first in Lake Geneva, Wisconsin and now in Stone Park, Illinois (literally a stone's throw from O'Hare). Women who are dazzled by the glitzy Las Vegas style show at Dana Montana's world famous **Sugar Shack II** swear there is nothing quite like it. Men say the same thing about **Heavenly Bodies,** a gentlemen's club in neighboring Elk Grove Village, featuring exotic female dancers almost round the clock.

Nightclubs

DESPERADOS
3860 25th Av
Schiller Park, IL   708 678-0033

Features: Country Western Bar
Transportation: Suburban Taxi from O'Hare $9

DUMAS WALTER'S
1799 S Busse Rd
Mt. Prospect, IL   708 593-2200

Features: County Western Bar
Transportation: Suburban Taxi from O'Hare $15

GASLIGHT CLUB
O'Hare Hilton
Opposite Terminal #2   312 686-0200

Features: Costumed waitresses
Transportation: Walk to Hilton opposite Terminal #2

HEAVENLY BODIES
1300 S Elmhurst Rd
Elk Grove Village, IL   708 806-1120

Features: More than 100 female models and table dancers
Transportation: Suburban Taxi from O'Hare $12

NASHVILLE NORTH
101 E Irving Park Rd
Bensenville, IL   708 595-0170

Features: Country Western Bar
Transportation: Suburban Taxi from O'Hare $17

SUGAR SHACK II
4003 Lake St
Stone Park, IL   708 343-9660

Features: Dana Montana's world famous exotic male dancers
Transportation: Suburban Taxi from O'Hare $10

SUNDOWNERS RANCH
3040 Mannheim Rd
Franklin Park, IL   708 451-6033

Features: Country Western Bar
Transportation: Any Taxi from O'Hare $8

WHITE NIGHTS
10290 W Higgins Rd
Rosemont, IL   708 824-3070

Features: Russian Nightclub
Transportation: Any Taxi from O'Hare $8

Dinner Theaters

DRY GULCH DINNER THEATER
9351 W Irving Park Rd
Schiller Park, IL   708 671-6644

Features: The theater presents a 2½ hour country western dinner/show package.
Transportation: Suburban Taxi from O'Hare $9

KING'S MANOR
2122 W Lawrence Av
Chicago, IL   312 275-8400

Features: Wenches serve drinks and a six course dinner as jesters, minstrels and magicians present a musical review.
Transportation: Chicago Taxi from O'Hare $20

Performing Arts Centers

ROSEMONT HORIZON STADIUM
6920 N Mannheim Rd
Rosemont, IL   708 559-1212

Features: The 18,000 seat auditorium has hosted circuses, rodeos, professional wrestling, ice dancing, college basketball and performances by The Grateful Dead, Paul McCartney, Jon Bon Jovi and others.

Transportation: Any Taxi from O'Hare $8

ROSEMONT O'HARE EXPO CENTER
5555 N River Rd
Rosemont, IL   708 318 6666

Features: The country's 12th largest convention/exposition center is host to craft shows, gardening shows, jewelry shows, golf shows, etc.

Transportation: Any Taxi from O'Hare $8, Subway $1.50

Horse Racing

ARLINGTON INTERNATIONAL RACECOURSE
Euclid & Wilke Rd
Arlington Heights, IL   708 255-4300

Features: Thoroughbred racing May through October

Transportation: Suburban Taxi from O'Hare $15

HAWTHORNE RACE COURSE
3501 Laramie Av
Cicero, IL   708 780-3700

Features: Harness racing January and February; Thoroughbred racing October through December.

Transportation: Any Taxi from O'Hare $20

MAYWOOD PARK RACE TRACK
8600 W North Av
Maywood, IL   708 343-4800

Features: Harness racing February through May and October through December.

Transportation: Suburban Taxi from O'Hare $15

SPORTSMAN'S PARK
3301 Laramie Av
Cicero, IL   312 242-1121

Features: Thoroughbred racing February through May; Harness racing May through October.
Transportation: Any Taxi from O'Hare $20

RECREATIONAL SPORTS

You don't have to skip your fitness routine because you're **STRANDED AT O'HARE.** Local fitness centers and suburban parks offer daily use of facilities for a nominal fee: exercise equipment, racquetball courts, indoor swimming pools, and during warm weather, outdoor swimming pools and tennis courts. From mid-March until the first snowfall, public golf courses welcome beginners and seasoned players. If your set of irons is in your garage and you are **STRANDED AT O'HARE,** don't worry, clubs are available for rent at these courses. And don't let darkness stop you, try an evening game at the **Ramada's lighted 9 hole course** in nearby Rosemont.

Note: The fitness center in the **O'Hare Hilton** is open to hotel guests only, O'Hare does not have public fitness facilities.

Fitness Facilities

BENSENVILLE PARK DISTRICT
1000 W Wood St
Bensenville, IL 708 766-7015

Facilities: Exercise facilities, golf, tennis, racquet ball.
Cost: Nominal daily fee.
Transportation: Suburban Taxi from O'Hare $17

BODY CLUB
1220 Mark St
Bensenville, IL 708 595-9009

Facilities: Racquetball, aerobics, whirlpool, sauna.
Cost: Nominal daily fee.
Transportation: Suburban Taxi from O'Hare $17

DES PLAINES PARK DISTRICT
2222 Birch St
Des Plaines, IL 708 391-5700

Facilities: Outdoor pool, tennis, golf.
Cost: Nominal daily fee.
Transportation: Any Taxi from O'Hare $12

ELK GROVE VILLAGE PARK DISTRICT
999 Leicester
Elk Grove Village, IL 708 437-9444

Facilities: Tennis.
Cost: Nominal daily fee.
Transportation: Suburban Taxi from O'Hare $12

FRANKLIN PARK PARK DISTRICT
9560 W Franklin Av
Franklin Park, IL 708 455-2852

Facilities: Outdoor pool.
Cost: Nominal daily fee.
Transportation: Suburban Taxi from O'Hare $8

NORDIC HILLS RESORT & CONFERENCE CENTER
Rt 53 and Nordic Rd
Itasca, IL   708-773-2750

Facilities: Racquet ball.
Cost: Nominal daily fee.
Transportation: Suburban Taxi from O'Hare $12

NORRIDGE PARK DISTRICT
4631 Overhill Av
Norridge, IL   708 457-1244

Facilities: Tennis, outdoor pool.
Cost: Nominal daily fee.
Transportation: Any Taxi from O'Hare $12

PARK RIDGE PARK DISTRICT
1515 Touhy Av
Park Ridge, IL   708 692-5129

Facilities: Exercise facilities, indoor pool, racquet ball.
Cost: Nominal daily fee.
Transportation: Any Taxi from O'Hare $12

ROSEMONT PARK DISTRICT
6140 W Scott St
Rosemont, IL   708 823-6685

Facilities: Tennis, racquet ball, indoor pool.
Cost: Nominal daily fee.
Transportation: Any Taxi from O'Hare $8

SCHILLER PARK PARK DISTRICT
9638 W Irving Park Rd
Schiller Park, IL   708 671-8580

Facilities: Racquet ball, tennis.
Cost: Nominal daily fee.
Transportation: Suburban Taxi from O'Hare $9

VETERAN'S PARK
24th and Cortez
Melrose Park, IL   708 343-5151

Facilities: Racquet ball.
Cost: Nominal daily fee.
Transportation: Suburban Taxi from O'Hare $15

YMCA
300 W Northwest Hwy
Des Plaines, IL   708 296-3376

Facilities: Racquet ball.
Cost: Nominal daily fee.
Transportation: Any Taxi from O'Hare $12

Golf Courses

BILLY CALDWELL GOLF COURSE
6150 N Caldwell Av
Chicago, IL   312 792-1930

Features: Open to the public, 9 hole course, club rental, pro shop, snack bar, no reservations accepted.
Transportation: Chicago Taxi from O'Hare $15

EDGEBROOK GOLF COURSE
6100 N Central Av
Chicago, IL   312 763-8320

Features: Open to the public, 18 hole course, pro shop, snack bar, club rental, reserved tee times.
Transportation: Chicago Taxi from O'Hare $15

FOX RUN GOLF LINKS
333 Plum Grove Rd
Elk Grove Village, IL   708 980-GOLF

Features: Open to the public, 18 hole course, pro shop, snack bar, club rental, reserved tee times.
Transportation: Suburban Taxi from O'Hare $12

INDIAN BOUNDARY GOLF COURSE
8600 W Forest Preserve Dr
Chicago, IL   708 366-9466

Features: Open to the public, 18 hole course, pro shop, snack bar, club rental, reserved tee times.
Transportation: Chicago Taxi from O'Hare $10

LAKE PARK GOLF COURSE
1005 Howard Av
Des Plaines, IL   708 391-5730

Features: Open to the public, 18 hole course, pro shop, snack bar, club rental, no reservations accepted.
Transportation: Any Taxi from O'Hare $12

MT. PROSPECT PARK DISTRICT GOLF COURSE
600 See Gwun Av
Mt. Prospect, IL   708 259-4200

Features: Open to the public, 18 hole course, snack bar, club rental, reserved tee times.
Transportation: Suburban Taxi from O'Hare $15

NORDIC HILLS RESORT & CONFERENCE CENTER
Rt 53 and Nordic Rd
Itasca, IL 708 773-2750

Features: Open to the public, 18 hole course, pro shop, snack bar, club rental, reserved tee times.
Transportation: Suburban Taxi from O'Hare $12

OLD ORCHARD COUNTRY CLUB
700 West Rand Rd
Mt. Prospect, IL 708 255-2025

Features: Open to the public, 18 hole course, pro shop, snack bar, club rental, reserved tee times.
Transportation: Suburban Taxi from O'Hare $15

RAMADA O'HARE GOLF COURSE
6600 N Mannheim Rd
Rosemont, IL 708 827-5131

Features: Open to the public, 9 hole course, pro shop, snack bar, club rental.
Transportation: Any Taxi from O'Hare $8

SALT CREEK GOLF CLUB
18 W 700 Thorndale Av
Wood Dale, IL 708 773-0184

Features: Open to the public, 9 hole course, pro shop, snack bar, club rental, reserved tee times.
Transportation: Suburban Taxi from O'Hare $17

WHITE PINES COUNTRY CLUB
500 W Jefferson Av
Bensenville, IL 708 766-0304

Features: Open to the public, two 18 hole courses, restaurant, club rental, reserved tee times.
Transportation: Suburban Taxi from O'Hare $17

SHOPPING

Have you run out of clean underwear? Do you want to replace a squashed suitcase? Whether you need to do some serious shopping or you just want to browse, you'll find a good selection of reasonably priced merchandise at suburban malls located near O'Hare.

GOLF MILL SHOPPING CENTER
Golf Rd & Milwaukee Av
Niles, IL					708 699-9440

Hours: 10–9 M–F, 10–5:30 Sat, 11–5 Sun
Features: More than 140 stores including J.C. Penney and Kohl's. Adjacent to several strip malls.
Transportation: Any Taxi from O'Hare $15

HARLEM IRVING PLAZA
4104 N Harlem Av
Norridge, IL					708 453-7800

Hours: M–F 10–9, Sat 9:30–9, Sun 11–5

Features: Over 125 stores including Kohl's, Carson Pirie Scott and Best Buy. Adjacent to smaller shopping malls.
Transportation: Any Taxi from O'Hare $15

WINSTON PLAZA
1254 Winston Plaza
(North Av and 9th Av)
Melrose Park, IL   708 343-9130

Hours: 10–5:30 M–F, 10-7 Sat, 10–5:30 Sun
Features: Approximately 80 stores including Marshall's.
Transportation: Suburban Taxi from O'Hare $15

PRACTICAL INFORMATION

Area Codes
Chicago (312); Suburbs (708)

Automated Banking Machines
Terminal #1, Concourse B; Terminal #2, Upper Level; Terminal #3, Upper Level.

Chapel
Terminal #2, Mezzanine Level.

Florist
O'Hare Hilton Hotel, Lower Level.

Lockers
(Machines require 4 quarters)
Terminal #2, near the following gates: E–1A, E–1, E–3, F–2 and in Terminal #3, near the following gates: G–2, G–10, G–14, H–4, H–5, K–4, L–2.

Lost & Found
If you lose something on an airplane call that airline but if you lose something in the airport call (312) 686-2200.

Lottery Tickets
(Twice Weekly Drawing of Millions)
Brightly colored booths are located in each terminal, Upper Level.

Money Transfer
Mutual of Omaha booths in Terminals #2 and #3 and Lower Level of O'Hare Hilton; also at the Independence Bank facilities in Terminal #3 and the International Terminal.

Shoe Repair
Terminal #1, Concourse B; and in Terminals #2 and #3, Upper Level.

Shoe Shine
Terminal #1, Concourses B and C; Terminal #2, Upper Level and Concourses E and F; Terminal #3, Upper Level and Concourses G, H and K.

Travellers Checks
Independence Bank booths in Terminal #3 and the International Terminal, (312) 686-7965; The Currency Exchange in Lower Level of the O'Hare Hilton, (312) 686-0180 and Mutual of Omaha office in the Lower Level of the O'Hare Hilton.

EMERGENCIES

Alcoholism
Alcoholics Anonymous 24 hour hotline (312) 346-1475.

Dentists
Chicago Dental Society 24 hour referral hotline (312) 726-4321. O'Hare Dental Group, Lower Level of O'Hare Hilton, office hours 8:30am-5pm, Monday through Friday, (312) 601-8900.

First Aid
First Aid Office in Terminals #2 and #3 (312) 686-2288.

Physicians
Chicago Medical Society Physician Referral Service (312) 670-2550. Schiller Park Medical Center (708) 678-6474. Free van from O'Hare.

Paramedics
Airport paramedics (312) 686-2244.

Pharmacies (Open 24 hours)
Osco Drug, 4732 N Pueblo, Chicago, IL (312) 625-5525; Walgreen Drug Store, 1828 S Cumberland Av, Park Ridge, IL (708) 696-0920.

Police
Call 911 or (312) 686-2230.

HOW TO ORDER THIS BOOK

STRANDED AT O'HARE
is available for $9.95
plus $2.50 shipping per
copy. (Add 6 1/4% sales tax for
deliveries within Illinois.)

Orders must be prepaid.
Please make your check payable to
"Stranded at O'Hare" and send your order to:

The Book Factory
P.O. Box 4430
Chicago, IL 60680-4430

This book is available at special
discounts when purchased in bulk for
promotions or premiums.

Customized corporate gifts can be
created in large quantities.